I0883008

UPDOG

DEADLY DISEASES

# Bubonic PLAGUE

## The Black Death

Percy Leed

Lerner Publications ◆ Minneapolis

Copyright © 2022 by Lerner Publishing Group, Inc.

All rights reserved. International copyright secured. No part of this book may be reproduced, stored in a retrieval system, or transmitted in any form or by any means—electronic, mechanical, photocopying, recording, or otherwise—without the prior written permission of Lerner Publishing Group, Inc., except for the inclusion of brief quotations in an acknowledged review.

Lerner Publications Company
An imprint of Lerner Publishing Group, Inc.
241 First Avenue North
Minneapolis, MN 55401 USA

For reading levels and more information, look up this title at www.lernerbooks.com.

Main body text set in ITC Franklin Gothic Std.
Typeface provided by Adobe Systems.

**Designer:** Mary Ross

**Library of Congress Cataloging-in-Publication Data**

Names: Leed, Percy, 1968– author.
Title: Bubonic plague: the black death / Percy Leed.
Description: Minneapolis : Lerner Publications , [2022] | Series: Deadly diseases (UpDog Books) | Includes bibliographical references and index. | Audience: Ages 8–11 | Audience: Grades 4–6 | Summary: "The bubonic plague wreaked havoc in the fourteenth century. Discover the symptoms behind the disease and what people did to slow the spread"— Provided by publisher.
Identifiers: LCCN 2020036283 | ISBN 9781728428352 (library binding) | ISBN 9781728430621 (ebook pdf)
Subjects: LCSH: Plague—Juvenile literature. | Black Death—Juvenile literature. | Epidemics—Juvenile literature.
Classification: LCC RA644.P7 L44 2022 | DDC 614.5/732—dc23

LC record available at https://lccn.loc.gov/2020036283

Manufactured in the United States of America
1-49372-49476-12/11/2020

# Table of Contents

# Plague!

The patient has a fever and chills. She also has a swollen neck.

Could it be bubonic plague?

Plague is most common in Asia, Africa, and South America.

It makes lymph nodes swell.

**lymph node:** a tissue that gets rid of waste in the body

It gives people fevers.

Fleas spread plague.

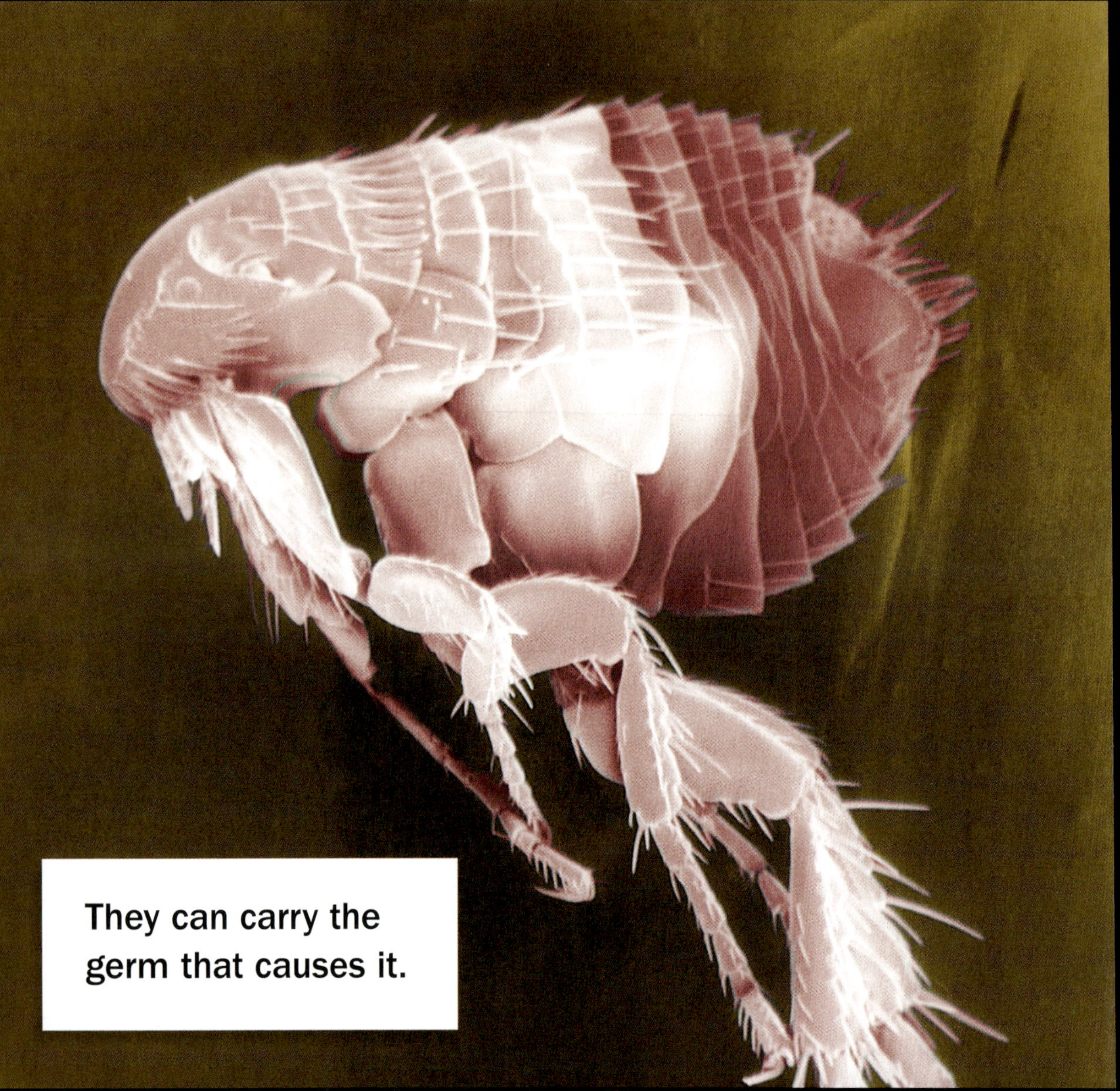

They can carry the germ that causes it.

## UP NEXT!

## The Black Death.

# Plague in the Past

The Black Death was a plague outbreak.

**outbreak:** a spread of disease

# UP CLOSE

The image on the right shows the plague germ.

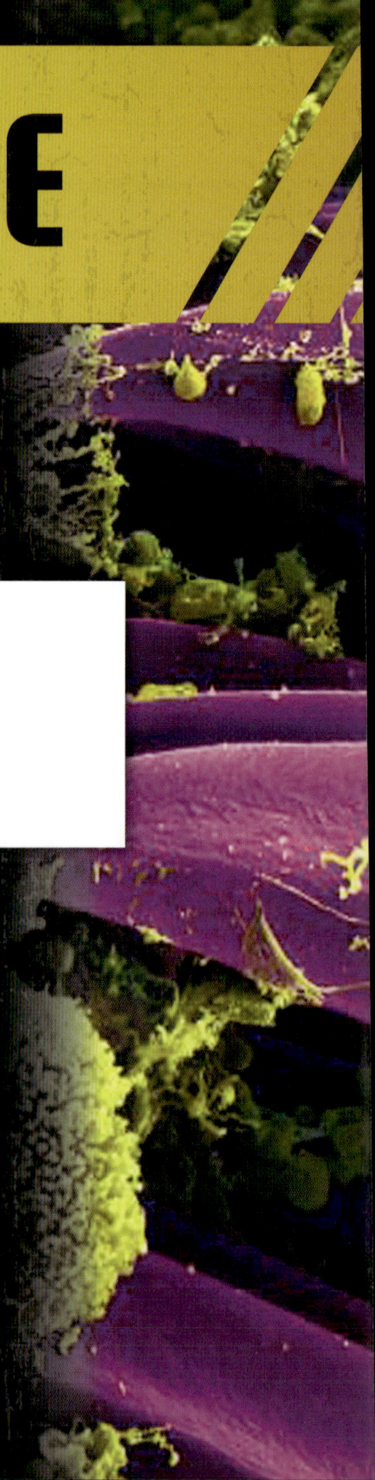

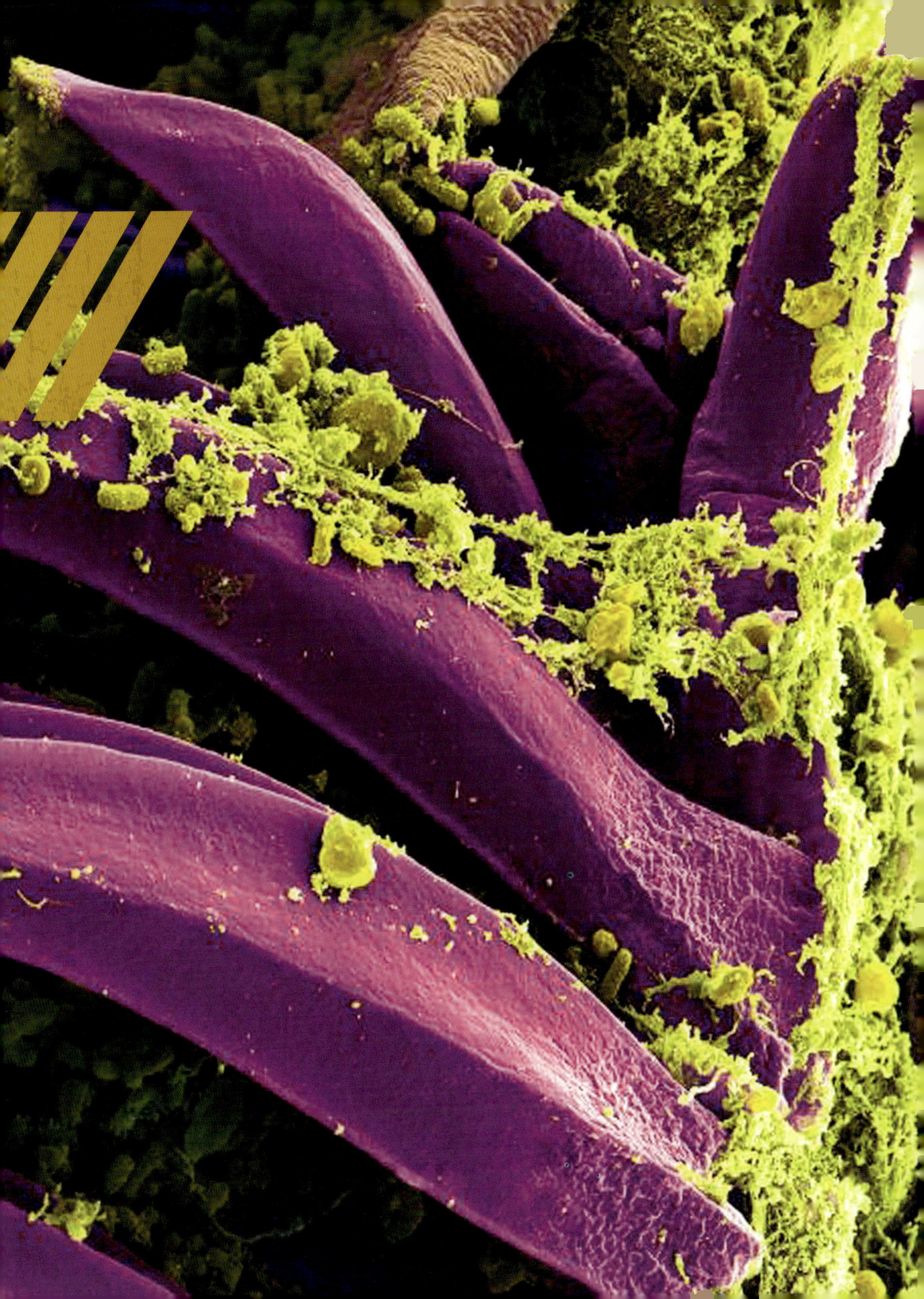

The Black Death happened in the 1300s.

It spread through Europe.

**Europe quarantined sick sailors.**

**quarantine:** to keep apart

This slowed the plague's spread.

## UP NEXT!
## Modern Times.

# Plague Today

Modern cities are cleaner.

Modern medicines work better. In countries where outbreaks happen, quarantines can help.

Plague is rare today.

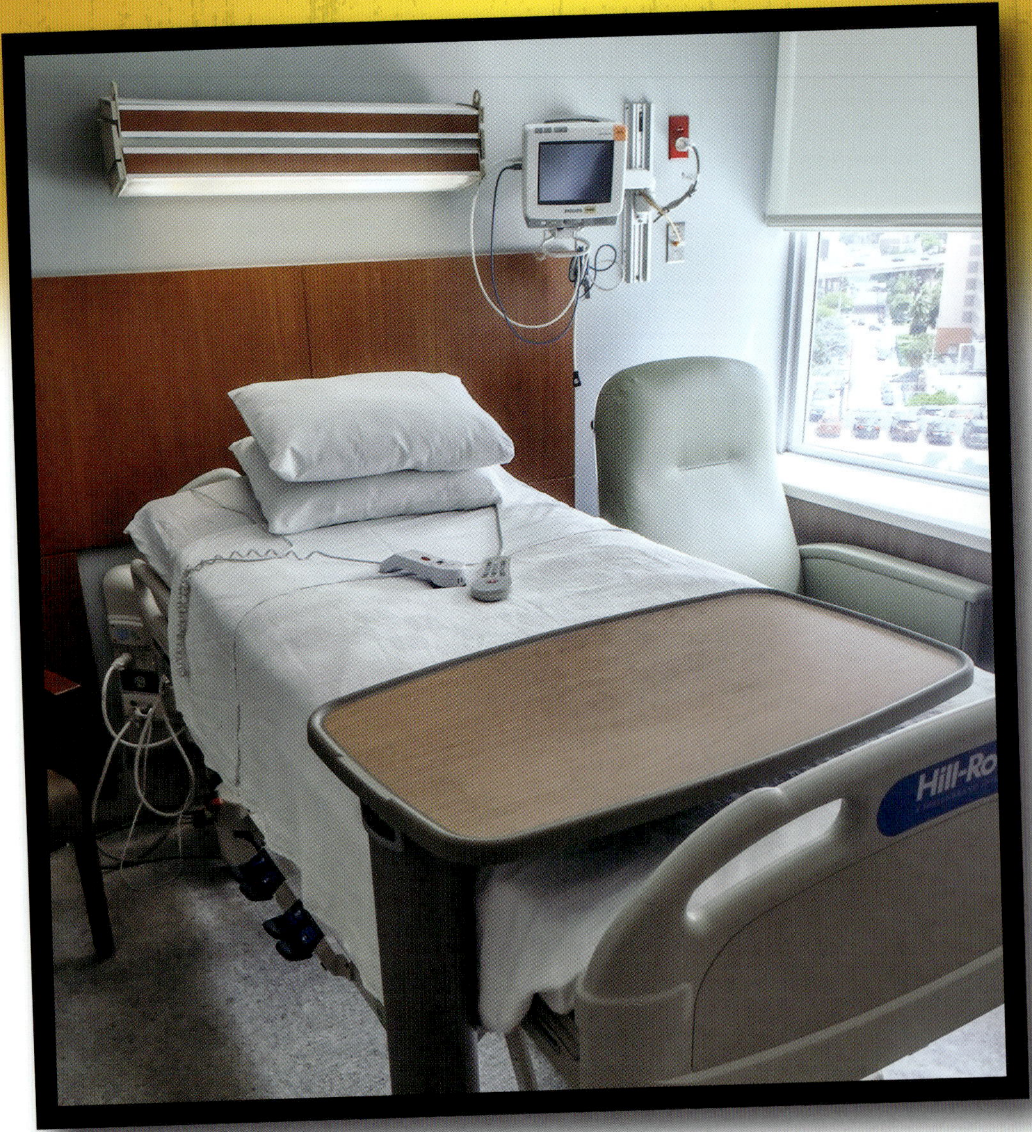

# DOCTOR YOU!

## Which patient do you think has the plague?

### Patient A

fever

chills

swollen lymph nodes

### Patient B

cough

fever

chills

Answer: Patient A

## Glossary

**lymph node:** a tissue that gets rid of waste in the body

**outbreak:** a spread of disease

**quarantine:** to keep apart

## Check It Out!

Alkire, Jessie. *Super Gross Germ Projects.* Minneapolis: Super Sandcastle, 2019.

Britannica Kids: Plague
https://kids.britannica.com/kids/article/plague/353636

Farndon, John. *Plague! Epidemics and Scourges through the Ages.* Minneapolis: Hungry Tomato, 2017.

Kiddle: Black Death Facts for Kids
https://kids.kiddle.co/Black_Death

KidsHealth: What Are Germs?
https://kidshealth.org/en/kids/germs.html

Mould, Steve. *The Bacteria Book.* New York: DK/Penguin Random House, 2018.

# Index



# Photo Acknowledgments


Image credits: Pormezz/Shutterstock.com, p. 4; Maxger/Shutterstock.com, p. 6; VILevi/Shutterstock.com, p. 7; Prostock-studio/Shutterstock.com, p. 8; Vera Larina/Shutterstock.com, p. 9; Everett Collection/Shutterstock.com, p. 10; Interfoto/Alamy Stock Photo, p. 11; National Institute of Allergy and Infectious Diseases, p. 13; Eugen Holländer/Wikimedia Commons (PD), p. 14; Jeffrey Coolidge/Getty Images, p. 15; Lanmas/Alamy Stock Photo, p. 16; Walker Art Library/Alamy Stock Photo, p. 17; f11photo/Shutterstock.com, p. 18; Dmytro Zinkevych/Shutterstock.com, p. 19; Rudy Umans/Shutterstock.com, p. 20.

Cover: royaltystockphoto.com/Shutterstock.com.